WINGED HORSES

BOOKS ALSO BY **PAUL ZEPPELIN**

Shattered Silence
Naked Trees
Evasive Paradise
Eternal Carnival
Fading Lights
Unpainted Portraits
Unknown Pathways
Sinless Mirrors
Burning Bridges
Sunlit Nights
Glass House

WINGED HORSES

PAUL ZEPPELIN

WINGED HORSES

iUniverse books may be ordered through booksellers or by contacting:

iUniverse
1663 Liberty Drive
Bloomington, IN 47403
www.iuniverse.com
844-349-9409

ISBN: 978-1-6632-7032-0 (sc)
ISBN: 978-1-6632-7033-7 (e)

Print information available on the last page.

iUniverse rev. date: 01/28/2025

Foreword

Paul Zeppelin writes his poetry as a passionate but convincing stream of bright ideas, intense emotions, and laconic clarity without any taboos, whatsoever. He comfortably writes about "Forbidden issues" as religions, sex, politics, and ethics. His verses unearth the deepest layers of our beliefs and doubts, of our dreams and hopes. There is an ancient proverb: "Only the mirrors are sinless."

Paul tried to be a "cold-blooded" mirror reflecting the world we dwell in, but quickly realized that his vibrant curiosity led him into a "no-way-out" labyrinth of, at times, dark conclusions about humans as such.

Being a pragmatic optimist, he often sees a ray of light at the end of his lifelong journey.

Judith Parrish Broadbent
Author of *Golden Days: Stories and Poems of the Central South and Beyond*

P.S. I am eager to mention that Paul never hides his admiration of Irish and Russian limericks, lullabies and counting rhymes.

Contents

Avid

There are no strangers
In my always heartfelt verses;
I am one of those avid angels
Who riding the winged horses...
The muses of high imagination,
The bridled stars of my elation.

Reminiscence

Two candles were burning on the table,
The flames were bright but yet unstable.

Apparently, it was enough:
It was a vivid reminiscence
Of my very first desire to love,
While hiding from my innocence
In yet mysterious concupiscence…

A Single Shelf

My library still has a single shelf:
A little bent, a little dusty…
A real echo of myself;
Though, I am a bit rusty.

My sleepless nights
Let me devour all those books-
The smartest wordy creatures…
I drowned in the ocean of delights.
I learned much more
Than my schoolteachers,
But no one kept the score.

Today, my views have broadened:
I see the skies
Beside the rainy clouds;
I see the crowds,
I hear their cries…
Their worries never end.

Flipped Cohen

I can no longer wait…
There ain't no cure for hate.
There ain't no cure for love;
Goodbye, I've had enough.

I died, the church's bell still rings;
A goddess Niki spread her wings
And led me to the sinless grounds
Of bliss, without hares and hounds,
To start my rather better part of life
Among the other souls…they thrive.

Good Day

A formidable adversary
Is quite encouraging, not scary;
I'd rather have fearless competitions
Than calmly choke my own ambitions.

And if I lose,
I'll caress my bruise.
A parabolic curve of my decline
Will not destroy but only chill my spine.
At ninety, it's very hard to be almighty,
At times, I spread my forgotten wings
And my old body flies and even sings.

I'd give myself a longer rope
Before I hang my life to dry:
I breathe; I live and hope
Good day is not goodbye.

Shelves

The world is not an unforgiving place,
It is just full of villains we hate to face.
I think this world is easily forgiving
If we could judge ourselves…

Our heroic tales will bend the shelves.

My Friend

Predictability he can no longer bear:
It is too hot; the streets are empty;
The sweetest smell of roses
Swirls close to cutely awkward poses
Of marble sculptures here and there.

In his pervasive hunt for imperfections
He even digs into the minuscule nuances;
He offers his suggestions and corrections
But gets entirely immaterial responses.

He is naïve perhaps, but he is a braggart,
He is a leading connoisseur of modern art;
Besides, he is the ancient history revealer.

And even more, he is my conscience healer.

Despair

After the end of all the ends
There are no foes or friends;
The reasons disappear,
The monsters sowed seeds of fear
Threw out babies with the bathwater
And cheered that awful slaughter...

My heart remembers all who passed,
But after my departure from the past,
After the white, black, red and gray,
I hardly stand on quaking feet of clay.

Dog Collar

I had become a happy scholar;
I burned my self-centered life
Into a gallant smooth routine;
There is no always angry wife
To yelp and get under my skin.

I threw my belittling dog collar.

Let Loose

Time broke a few young twigs,
Time cut a few long branches,
Time ploughed a few tranches,
Then filled them with the pigs.

That wasn't time's best choice,
There is no reason to rejoice…

War came. The fragile peace
Had disappeared once more.
The gentle souls of our fallen
Are looking for a place to soar.

War is a grandiose black hole,
It is a terrifying, hungry beast,
It is an overwhelming monster,
That rises on fermenting yeast
Of our let loose inherited disaster.

Catch 22

Time was by all parameters insane,
Time hid the footprints of my deeds;
Only the foggy shadows still remain
Someplace perhaps along the weeds.

Swiftly arrived the wingless angels,
The agents of hatred and revenges;
They have arrived out of breath
To choke my vigilance with tricks,
But not to comfort me near death;
They craved my excellent antiques.

My deep anthropological research
Tried to examine our long coexistence;
It sent me back to my corrupted church,
And never offered eloquent assistance.

A Whiff

The good ole door sings in my house,
Dry and old-fashioned hinges squeak.

Being quite bored, I brought a lovely girl:
I wanted her to be a lucky second mouse
And let her ride my standing by joystick.

I must confess, she was a star, a pearl;
I couldn't guess what's in the box…
She was a perfect Goldilocks.

At dawn, she left a whiff of her perfume
In my routinely lonely and nasty gloom.

Meritocracy

Let's start;
Please, keep in mind
We aren't smart,
We're just forever blind.

Despite my futile efforts,
In spite of our legal courts,
The unions of hypocrisy
Destroyed our meritocracy...

Shaped a bloodthirsty predator,
Still a bit kinder than my editor.

Imprisoned

When consciences disturbed
Our decisions are unreasoned,
Our wills and hopes are curbed,
And hearts are cruelly imprisoned.

Wisdom birthed stupidity,
Death carved infinity,
Insanity created reasons,
Good chiseled evil,
Love nurtured hate,
Water provided droughts,
A tunnel ended with a light...

It never stops. Goodnight...

The most annoying rings of my cellphone
Returned me to a daily ride,
I heard a voice: your ex committed suicide.
Something had died in me,
Although, life has to go on,
Most likely, I will never soar to glee.

Actors Reenact

I saw the boneyard roses,
I saw the weeping poses,
I saw the grimaces of sorrows,
I saw the loneliest tomorrows…

I've seen it all too many times
As punishments without crimes.

Years passed,
I heard the church's bell:
The tombstones cracked,
The marble sculptures fell,
The sun moved to the west;

At dawn, these actors reenact

I promised to survive,
I pledged to stay alive...

Halleluiah

My wound was timely healed,
I walked across the battlefield,
Along the newly planted trees,
All of a sudden, a mild breeze,
A gentle wind woke up to blow;
I heard a tiny daisy murmured,
He loves me, he loves me not;
I heard the grass quietly grow.

A cuckoo bird chirped marches,
While the rainbow seven arches
Bent over the half-rainy heaven
Then each of those hued seven
Sang Leonard Coen's Halleluiah;
The hymn of life; the last hurrah.

The sun pierced sleepy overcast
Like a new idea through the past.

Escaped

I am tired; I am getting old;
Life teaches, I am enrolled;
I am still eager to retrieve
What sheepishly escaped.
My doubts haven't gone;
But I am not naïve.
O am not uncontrolled...
I see a baby-dawn,
My window isn't draped.
My future has begun.

Merriment

I hope all melancholic clouds
Become the happy rays of sun
Caressing our fertile grounds,
Healing the hearts of everyone.

This world will surely outlive me.
I promise you I won't be back,
Not as a reminder of our hilarity,
Not as a godsend blinding glory,
Not as a pebble from the quarry,
Not as a life-bringing ray of light
Flaunting its gimmicks on a site…

I won't disturb your peace,
I'll die in merriment of bliss.

Torches

Our nights are bright as torches,
Our days are light as butterflies;
We meet to smoke on our porches
And our problems quickly downsize.

My life is an unending honeymoon:
I will be ninety pretty soon,
Somedays, I dance or making love,
I weekly go to my gym to exercise,
Perhaps in vain, I hope it is enough
To put on hold my imminent demise.

Ducks and Drakes

Another waterfall,
Another rainy autumn,
I ran, I didn't drop the ball,
I ran, I didn't hit the bottom.
Another snowfall,
Another chilly winter,
I ran, I didn't have the ball,
I ran alone, I am a sprinter.

The nonexistent real truths
Had never seen our youths;
We ran...but our shoulders
Will drag Sisyphus' boulders.

Life is a game of ducks and drakes,
Without rules, but with hefty stakes.

Good Mothers

The hands of our mothers
Made from tenderness,
The arms ae made from love;
Their feelings are wholly effortless,
There are some good-willed others
Who love and care but not enough.

Good mothers
Cannot teach you
To be happy;
Good mothers
Teach you
To deserve your glee;

From time to time,
Recall the Holy Three.

The Thumb

The thumb of God is always on the scale,
The promised our free will doesn't exist,
Although, I clench my hand in fist,
The sinless smoothly sail,
The sinners slowly crawl
To reach the day of our creation,
To hear the primal sacramental word,
To touch the cradle of our stagnation,
To see the dawn of our hopeless world.

Rattles

My innocence hurled quarters:
Some wound up in fountains,
Some drowned in the oceans,
Some climbed the mountains;
Some hid in pockets of reporters;
I haven't showed my emotions:
I am sure, my innocence returns,
The bridge to nowhere never burns.

My strongest enemy is death;
No less and certainly no more;
I was victorious in many battles,
But I am defeated in the final war;
Because, although, out-of-breath,
The tail of a nasty snake still rattles.

In the aftermath of earthly life,
I went into a much better one,
I pledged my soul to my ex-wife,
I vowed not to be ever outdone.

Platoon

Platoon was twenty in the morning,
There are only ten of us at night;
War isn't just a friendly warning;
War is a never-ending hellish fight.

The tunnel is too long,
I am too old to wait
For a magic second it must end
And I will see the fated light;
I lost my dreams and hopes;
I am a boxer on the ropes
I lost my lifelong fight.

I lived. The night is hurling stars
Over the dense horizon's darkness,
I am still burning money in the bars,
Enjoying the minty mojito's tartness.

Nail Head

Life wants me to forget so very much:
Forget the luscious wines and dinners,
Forget that our good and evil go Dutch,
Forget the mobs of undeserving winners.

The sense of hunger was returning,
The candles were already burning,
I went to buy some fated daily bread,
The door was locked; the closing time;
Although, I'd hate to waste my rhyme,
It hurt; my hammer missed a nail head.

The spectacle was masterfully staged
The proven and old-fashioned way,
With a few real, eager actors:
A head of John the Baptist on the tray,
A feisty, go-getting dance; no outrage
Amid the beneficiates and benefactors.

Dejection

As admiral, I had a great career,
The rest were only vise or rear...

Young, brave and tough,
I used to telegraph
My dreams, desires, and hopes;
Today, I am a boxer on the ropes.

I am alone, continually followed
By my own shadow and my dog;
Without them my life is hollowed
Like a termite-eaten rotten log...

There is a newer mortal sin,
Our low-spirited dejection;
Instead of God's objection
It looks like the devil's win...

Without Crime

The Oldman sent it from above:
We learn pre-not- enough:
We learn pre-history,
We learn pre-mystery,
We learn pre-love,
We learn pre-time…

It started from the fallen angel;
First punishment without crime.
The Oldman was too vain
And pride has clouded his brain.

Today,
It's all about those three men
Who came to see the manger;
Today,
It's all about that bright star
That lured them from afar…

Morsels

My relevance is undisputed;
I write, somebody always reads;
Only my critics, being too stupid,
Destroy the sowed by me seeds.

In premonition of the red sunset,
That horrid messenger of Mars,
The mean ambassador of threat
To my beloved stars-and-bars,
Has reaffirmed my motto-mission:
Don't ever lie to our young,
Don't poison our tomorrows…
Their songs may die unsung…
And drown in the seas of sorrows.

My limericks and parables,
My deeply heartfelt verses,
At times, are mighty pearls,
At times, are futile rubbles,
But studded with the morsels
After the vigorous rehearsals.

Tasteless Charm

Our world is a huge pawnshop;
Yet, our globe is slowly turning
And doesn't want to stop
Amazing money earning…

My readers always know
How the poems grow-flow
From the manure of searches
Among the whores in churches
Despite their tasteless charm…

Which rhyme is still alive
Or quickly bought the farm.

Life often is the darkest mistral,
At times, it is the purest crystal.

Lark

My difficult, worn-out life is older
Than my already shattered soul,
But only the eye of the beholder
Perfectly reflects it as a whole.

I hope the word Apocalypse
Won't ever leave God's lips.

I am carving yet another fable
At my has-seen-this-movie
Exhausted plywood shaky table;
The rhymes are rather groovy;
I am goofily happy like a lark…

Why is my story so damn dark?

Scaffold

If I am made in your own image,
Why do you mess with me?
If you are so immensely strong
Just stop our bloody scrimmage;
End wars and we will get along,
End wars and we will know glee.

Please, use your mighty heart,
Don't ever use your morbid wit,
Don't separate us far apart
For those who always serve
And those who drink and eat;
Create delight we all deserve.

They rushed me to the scaffold
To hang, to shoot, to barbecue;
For what and why, I had no clue.
Goodbye. I haven't been paroled.

Our

I saw her as a glass half empty,
That glass was probably half full;
She used me as the Horn of Plenty,
But I was just a young and horny bull.

At times, our loves are dire
In *our* fully blinded passion;
We ruthlessly destroy *our* compassion
And all of what *our* loving hearts desire.

We scream; all *our* hands on deck,
But *our* cruiser is just a total wreck.

Heinous

Our intimidating menace
Will need to outlive us all,
So even the Wailing Wall
That whispers our wishes
Into the ears of a lazy god,
Won't send a lightning rod
To crack the empty dishes
Of our self-admiring faces.

For my taste fairly heinous.

Burials

To hate somebody far is easy,
To hate somebody near is hard;
Even our nods are sad and breezy
During the burials in our graveyard.

Don't ever try to fool your death,
Gods, let you push the boulders;
In war, don't gift your final breath
To careless greedy powerholders.

Time won't erase the scars of war.
Time quickly starts the other one.
I asked what are we fighting for?
Gods didn't bite the bait;
We had created you to hate;
The battles won't be ever gone.

Spittle

I never preach
To the converted;
I preach to the perverted
I pile the mud and bleach.

Oh, what a shame
To know very little,
But see your name
Polished with spittle.

I went beyond myself,
Beyond the boundaries of reason,
I left my cozy unassuming shelf,
I left the lifetime comfortable prison.

I didn't lose my final battle,
The tails of human snakes still rattle,
It is the nightly elegy of breath;
It is the looming enemy; it is my death.

A Bugle Playing

I hate to argue with this cretin,
He thinks the same of me,
Only our morbid egos threaten
To reach the promised glee.

Forget the ins and outs
Of our Apostles' creed,
The only truths and doubts
Allow the ancient fossils bleed.

My life is pain.
In vain, I push it to the limit,
Do I deserve to win it?
I am happy as a picnic basket
Until my dreams collapse,
Until I hear above my casket
A bugle playing farewell taps
To recollect, not to complain.

My train has drifted
And finally derailed.
It slid into a cul de sac,
Far from the morals scripted.
The Book as always failed
To put me on a lighter track.

My gun is waiting
For the final draw,
I am still debating
Whether it's a flaw.

Vigor

I live and write in silence
Away from so-called science
And so-called evenhanded news,
Away from doctors and their views.

I must admit, I read the news
A few days later; about two or four;
Facts change; I change my views,
And write much better than before.

Regrettably, I learned to cry:
I miss my critics, I fought but feared
I don't believe they all could die,
They simply disappeared…
And yet, with every bit of vigor
I write about all of them,
I want my verse to be much bigger
Than I am.

The Disarray of Thoughts

The more you know,
The less you sleep;
Life is a funny, witty show,
Why do you always weep?

A sign on the stairs to bliss:
Don't use this staircase
It leads to the abyss,
To our mortal sins birthplace.

The darkest light of education
Makes monsters for the masses;
Their trains have left the station
They have to ride their asses…

Red sunset fell to the abyss,
I couldn't stop the universe;
I tried but couldn't cease
The flow of my verse…

A sign of horoscope
Is a traditional tightrope
Across the Milky Way
From birth to my decay.

There is a tree of love,
There is a tree of hatred;
But at the end hereof,
Only the black, white, pale, and red.

We gather our support
In murmurs of the crowds
We reap ovations after bouts,
We see the blinding lightning rods,
We hear the thunders of the clouds,
In vain, we even calculate our odds
Before appearing in the traffic court.

I miss the red sunset
Since we have met,
I miss my birthright poise,
I miss your gentle voice
Descending from above,
There aint no cure for love.

Those who are "in the know"
Are waiting for their luck to glow,
But settle for big hats, no cattle;
Lose wars, win every battle...

I am redefining creativity,
I am reinventing my naiveté.
Ideas swirling in the heavens,
They are those viruses
That rest, but never die,
They are the drawbridge of sky.

Intelligence creates our sadism
Sophisticated and refined;
It is our constant escapism
Into the bliss that gods designed.

Winged horses
Left the skies,
My humble verses
Tensely agonize...
I am connecting stubborn dots,
And rhyme some newest thoughts.

I am reluctant to accept
The nervous rhythms of modernism;
I would prefer the streams of nihilism
The up-to-the-minute youth has kept.
Despite the riot of my ancient soul,
I watch the future thru an old keyhole.

Instead of a long dark walk
Into my complicated past...
I simply grabbed a piece of chalk
And outlined my flesh half-assed.

I pulled my vodka from the fridge,
It was the only remedy at hand,
Reliable, but totally unplanned;
Just like an ancient drawbridge.

I'd rather be sued by twelve
Than carried by the gloomy six;
I promised to defend myself
From filthy tongues of critics...

My room is flooded with sunshine,
The old alarm-clock rings insanely,
As always, cruelly and inhumanly...
I am in bliss; this is my cloud nine.

The heavy yoke
Of imminent despair
Is like a scorching sun
That burns a country fair;
Just like a yellow sopping yolk,
Exactly like my future one-on-one.

I was in pain, I moaned,
I walked the slope of my depression;
She was a goddess of compassion,
We kissed then both got stoned…

We are too bored in our corners,
We go outside to kiss the ugly frogs;
They morph into sad mourners
And grieve under the cats and dogs.

The star has shown them the way,
And every wise man-stranger
Was led to see the sacred manger
To give the gifts, to kneel and pray.

The crying babies ignored my sleep,
My plane ignored the heavy clouds,
I didn't ignore but tried to overleap
My fear of flying and sticky doubts.

Hailstorms
Don't wake the students' dorms,
The rainy heavens hurling stars
Into the windows opened wide,
Nobody is inside,
The kids are drinking in the bars.

A young bartender
Refused to serve me,
I hardly hold my vomit;
Close to my girl's rear fender,
I liked the godsend glee,
And never tired of it.

Too bad, my shrink abruptly said,
You have a silent agony of fear;
You need to have a case of beer,
Some salty nuts and a good friend.

I love the fiery sun of Paris,
I love the rainy clouds of Seattle,
But most of all I love my terrace,
My Guinness and a lazy tittle-tattle.

I write and never know when to fold,
The author's copy goes to a shelf;
The rest are hardly ever sold.
Am I still writing only for myself?

I Liaised

I liaised between rooftops
Without yields and stops…
I saw, in his lifelong despair
Sisyphus pushed the rocks
Across the airborne horizon.
Without bowing in a prayer,
My chances definitely rising
In chasing the Golden locks.

The autographs of war
Are carved on our souls
By wounds and sutures.
I wish our foggy futures
Will happily forever soar
Above the boneyards' walls…

Over the seeds we sowed,
Under the skies that wept,
The angels lazy and inept
Lost principles we owned.

Although, the stubborn doves
Still hold the olive branches;
The wars even in velvet doves
Don't let us leave the trenches.

Ecclesiastes

If you want peace, prepare for war;
In Latin, Si vis pasem, para bellum!
No small ideas anymore:
It's death or life; it's war or peace...
The great foreseer King Solomon
Created his Ecclesiastes,
And charted a lifetime road to bliss:
From your mother's cozy womb
Into your rather frigid tomb.
Enjoy your life, fear God...
Be careful, avoid His lighting rod...

There is a time to tear apart,
There is a time to sew together,
There is a time to speak,
There is a time for silence,
There is a time for war,
There is a time for peace,
There is a time to hate,
There is a time to love...
There is a time for all of the above.

Hypnos

I write in aromatic language
Most of my awkward verses;
This poem is an open sandwich
With fragranced truffle morsels.

I worked until midnight,
My tired head fell on a cheek
Of my beloved softest pillow;
My mind refused to fall asleep:
One more tormented edgy night;
Even a lazy Hypnos-god of sleep,
Is like a weeping willow
Can't stop its ceaseless weep...

Let me remind you anyway,
I often sleep during the day.

Curtain Raiser

Our souls hold seeds
Of what we'll become;
Our inner darker side
Is like a curtain raiser
For festivals of good and evil
For our unceasing trailblazer.

God made the Milky Way,
Then went *God knows where.*
To take his darkness far away,
Where my light side laid bare;
To generate the newer worlds,
To say the other primal words.

He gifted me ability to change
The verse I want to rearrange…

Victors

I wasn't given the hero's parts
In our life on the drama's stage;
I dove into the family of arts,
And never turned the other page.

I hope, I'll gleam one day;
Get ready-I'm on the way.

The only history we know
Was written by the victors;
The days imagined by predictors
Are unattractive but try to glow...
Our almighty elegantly chaffing,
Even the grim reality is laughing.

All quiet on the western front,
Lulled by the absurdity of war,
Continuously painful and blunt,
While death is waiting at the door.

Greed Governs

The good ole' money
Makes days quite sunny.

Greed governs our lives,
No fights in our defense;
I hope beyond the fence
Our decency still thrives.

We are either predators or prey;
Those born to crawl will never fly;
That is our predestined way;
Don't change. Don't even try!

The naves of any church
Are ships of fools;
Arks of salvations
Filled with the loud mules.
Quite lovely congregations.

Gods locked the heaven's gates;
It is a penalty for their crusades;

Misery

They sentenced me
To twenty years of boredom
As Leonard Cohen claimed;
I climbed Saint Peter's Dome;
My life's sunset already flamed
To burn my never promised glee.

My luck was sliding,
Hitting the steps of a stairway
From the evasive ancient bliss
Into the fiery welcoming abyss.
St. Peter and St. Paul were hiding
Behind the planets of the Milky Way.

The known world is crumbling,
No one can hear our futile cries,
Above the oceans' everlasting ice,
Our decency and morals disappear,
Our conscience trembling in its fear
Only the young mindlessly snuggling.

Catharsis

I am a wizard, I turn the tricks:
I pull the rabbits from the hats,
I catch the falling knifes,
I blow fires off the wicks,
I train the mice to love the cats;
Just like a cat, I have nine lives.

I relish my unnecessary rhymes,
And yet, I wander in the weeds,
With aspirations and with needs
To resurrect my literary crimes.

A man is the shortest bridge
Connecting wisdom and stupidity,
Connecting heavens with infinity,
Connecting suffering with dignity.

Baroque

Beethoven always talked to me,
The others often passed me by;
They'd turn their heads away:
Never hello, neither goodbye...
But I still tried to play...

I tried to play a hidden
Exercise in mathematics:
Adventurous but not forbidden
The sound-ridden acrobatics...

The last sonata of Beethoven,
The enigmatic thirty two...
I froze like a nomadic Bedouin
Who never heard of morning dew.

It was a divine perfection
Lamenting for the dead...
It was enormity of resurrection,
A marble set of steps ahead...

The final diamond of the Baroque...

I learned to play that masterstroke.

Horsemen

I keep my ear close to ground,
I leave my fingerprints around,
I wonder if it helps or hinders…
Meanwhile, my hunt still lingers
For four apocalyptic horsemen,
Who didn't show up back then…

During that horrid spring's amazing rite,
When was crucified the Prince of Light,
When a deep darkness had descended,
When the most precious life has ended.

My Granny's Globe

I'm just an uninvited guest in my own home.
The roof and walls don't shield me anymore,
As of a;; kids had gone to high school prom,
But I'm biting nails and waiting at the door.

I pawned my granny's globe
With borders rearranged by endless wars,
With ancient cities' names changed,
With a few countries gone forever,
With friends and enemies that vanished,
But left behind the churches' whores.

Dreams disappeared in a cacophonic hymn,
Filling the town's moonshine barrel to its rim.
They jumped into the whirlpool of nightmares
To swim between the conmen and their heirs.

A new chaotic time hangs on the leafless trees.
Only the looting gangs enjoy their filthy expertise.

I grabbed my old grenade and tossed it to the room,
Then calmly watched…the sunshine didn't fade.
I only heard a loud, ears bursting boom.
That's all. It was a lovely show. No one paid.

Don't interrupt my dire nightmare; I'm in the white-hot hell;
It is a fated, prearranged affair. I hit the bottom of the well.

Contacts

Not many friends alive
Left in my cellphone contacts,
But I still call them every day.
Send them a message or a fax.
Trying to react them in bliss
Or the abyss
Of our endless Milky Way.

I learned to understand
The convoluted alphabet
Of tasteless shorter rings.

Our friendships are alive and fly
On never resting mighty wings;
We never say goodbye.

Four

I drink the wine of sorrow
To a good luck tomorrow...

The tasty meals and lavish wines
Cross-pollinated with my friends,
And wandering across the world
To figure out if the horizon bends
Take to the bank my honest word,
And never read the warning signs.

These are my four life baring morsels.
Great meals, wines, friends, and trips;
Unlike the final horses of apocalypse
They are my muses, my flying horses.

Passages

These words are true to my own story,
They trace the passages of my emotions,
Their timid failures and their vivid glory.
Their quiet havens and their wild oceans.

Some journeys take a minute,
Some others take lifetimes;
Imagination has no limit;
I soured above my rhymes…

I never wrote a boring daily diary;
I wrote a grim obituary to life I lived
That was exuberantly bright and fiery;
Reflected in the rhymes I weaved.

The wings of a fallen Lucifer
Don't block the sun from me;
I permanently circle every square
In premonition of my endless glee.

Intuition

My optimistic spirits
Cheerlessly fell and drowned
In mercilessly coldblooded rivers;
The hell descended to the ground.

Our train moved from a station LOVE
Into a dismal station named DIVORSE,
Ending the better and the worse
As being sworn to someone far above.

A torture was a pleasing habit
Of our, created in His image, kind,
And a refined, exquisite hatred
Left our inborn kindness far behind.

My mind can make a mistake;
My intuition-never;
I give or take, care or forsake…
My heart remains forever clever.

Prophets

Good poets are those prophets,
That weren't ever heard
By worshipers of bloody profits,
But never of the primal word.

Catastrophe arrives without a reason,
Just like a bright charisma of sunrise;
I run into a self-inflicted mental prison
Away from every unsolicited advice…

When I can't find happiness,
I look at the simple people;
They throw themselves
Into the arms of fate…

I envy them, but I am not simple;
I learned a lot; for me it is too late.

I'll Pay Off My Debits

I'll forget my habits;
I'll forget my past;
I'll pay off my debits;
I'll fade without a blast.

Life is a theater of the absurd.
A stage is dark, I lit a chandelier.
Two daughters joined the cast.
The future is completely blurred.
Am I a gentle gullible King Lear,
Or just a glimmer from the past?

By early morning, I'll be gone.
The threshold sees my shadow.
My crown will be theirs at dawn.
The world may see its afterglow.

What is in the name?
I am invited into bliss.
The solace of my fame
Gave me a farewell kiss.

Eternity will judge my life
And run it through a murky sieve.
Life is a cruel perpetual midwife.
She brings new days; we grieve.

Orbits

We all have our own orbits;
They intermingle and overlap;
Some fly, some fall into the pits.
Some flip, some choose to flip.

We praise our mindless bravery.
We glorify our thoughtful humility.
We wrap them in a silky drapery
Of our steadily acquired gentility.

We navigate the sea of sameness.
It seems as if we are completely aimless.
Although we see the end of our despair,
The better days are right upon us,
Forthcoming like the lazy pandas.

We are forever blinded by their glare.

Nearby

The words of history veer in the air,
And if we'll ever read and learn,
The so-called sinners will not burn,
The so-called angels will not fly...
There are no saints and sinners,
Only the losers and the winners
Within confines of our universe;
I will be there, somewhere nearby
To write a new, much better verse.

I am close to being ninety,
My skills are somewhat honed;
Turns out, I am not Shakespeare,
I am not that fruitful and mighty ...
I didn't fume; I only sadly moaned,
Still write, but changed the gear.

Humanoids

I didn't learn Greek comedies
In the red-brick-ivied-schools,
I lived through real tragedies
Created by the human fools.

I taught there once or twice before,
And realized that a state college
Provides a bit of carnal knowledge,
But shamefully not much more.

They quickly showed me the door.

Today, I hung a poster in my digs:
"No humanoids-I prefer the pigs!"

Ripened

The dust of times
Still hanging in the air,
Descending on my rhymes,
Then lead them to nowhere.

I went beyond the WHAT
To comprehend the WHY;
My brain looks like a walnut,
But I'm no more a passerby.

I never needed inspirations,
The new ideas dwell in me,
I let them leave the stations
To share their ripened glee.

I am a bird held by the nets,
I try to pay my heavy debts:
I write then wipe my shoes
On every insincere excuse.

Almighty Puppeteer

We never see the roots,
We only watch the surface blooms,
We march across in our dirty boots,
While the inevitable judgement looms.

The snow melts beneath our feet:
We are still marching down here,
Jerked by the almighty puppeteer
That doesn't let us choose the beat.

We hold the wrong end of the world equation,
We hold the erratic see-saw of good and evil,
Expecting nothing but a dire upheaval
In our pursuit of the most devious evasion
By those who have to lead and guide,
By the corrupted angels of the darkest kind.

Our struggle isn't ending,
Those wingless angels never fly,
But look at us and callously demanding:
"Hang them high!"

Mist

I lived in dusty downtown dungeons,
I puffed the smoky air of artists' lofts,
My skinless blustery sub conscience
Would echo liberals and other "softs",
And whisper: "A verse is just a dream,
It's a wholehearted but unruly stream
Of peaks or valleys. No one to blame".

If the Olympic gods exist,
Reality is just a poetic mist;
It is a shameless need of fame.

To Ernest

Life is a running of the bulls,
No kindness and no rules,
It's a volcano ready to erupt,
Extremely deadly and abrupt.
It's not a feast that follows you
It's just a dangerous dark alley,
It's not a sunlit, lovely avenue.

It's just a show with a vile finale.

USA

I love my good ole USA
Without reservation,
Without any hope
To lead this nation
To yet another glorious V-day
With an idea, not a horoscope;
With our greatest constitution…
Without yet another civil war,
Without yet another revolution.

Our future's worth fighting for!

Frank

In French it's Comme il Faut,
Behave and go with the flow.

Last day in Paris, France:
A girl is trembling under me,
I am in bliss, I am in trance;
She cries: Mon Dieu, qui, qui.

Today, I am hands down frank,
Paris is always in my heart:
Left bank, Right bank...
The lovely ladies, food and art.

Decay

I crashed revolts of my rogue conscience,
Revolts of my confessions and remorses,
Revolts of friends that makes no sense
Revolts of boneyards with their corpses.

Life fused our bitter jealousy
With triumph and retaliation,
With the most intricate verbosity
To praise my poisoned jubilation.

In my nightmare, last night,
My conscience said,
I am the Lord inside of you,
I am your promised daily bread;
Without me there is no light,
There is no end to your decay…
Is this OK?

Neptune

Fish rot from the head down,
God Neptune has no shoes to lose;
I bet, he'll dump his royal crown
If he will get a chance to choose...

I try to comprehend the gods' desires,
I swim the waters; I jump through fires.

I think, as many heads as many minds;
In French: autant de tetes que d'esprits;
Some yank the threads,
Some kindly set us free.

Quartet

Life is a fruit, life is a child
Of the most grim love makers;
Expected and hardly ever wild,
A dreary world of undertakers.

Our life is a predicted paradigm
That has no mountains to climb;
The elder gods decayed already,
The times are cloudlessly steady.

A genius has chaos in his mind,
He dumped the paradigm behind:
For him the Trinity is not enough,
He wants to add AI,
He needs a powerful Quartet...
I disagree, but who am I?

I wonder who will pay the debt.

Shallow

A man is a result of his own reading:
If you don't read, your brain will die,
And it will never cast a shadow;
You live alone, boring, and shallow
Then whisper your goodbye.

You are exactly like the grass:
You quickly grow up, kick ass,
Get burned and slowly bend,
Then wilt, get delicate and dry,
Admit the guilt, accept the end,
And whisper your goodbye.

Revelation

The rich and poor are equal
When they are in their graves,
The Satan probably would kill;
Is there someone who saves?

I wouldn't give my mind
A well-deserved vacation:
Each of my written verse
Derives from my remorse,
Disguised as a revelation.

It's easy to fall in love
With total strangers,
It's awfully hard to love
The one near you...
I love the passed by angels;
They're no longer in my view.

Suffering

Religions wrecked themselves,
They never learned the primal word,
The prophets collect dust on shelves,
The holy spirit is a lifelong jailbird.

The Book is written to glorify the past,
To justify the myths about all the rest;
It is the act of faith; it is Auto-da-fe,
It is a merciless punishment of glee...

They say, without suffering
You won't appreciate the truth...
I say, the truth is a recovering
Of our innocence in youth.

Dialectics

I am observing dialectics
Of the opposing powers,
Wide-ranging yet eclectic:
The hot and cold,
The dirt and gold,
The sun and wilted flowers.

I don't enjoy our awful times
Of sentences without crimes.

I walk and run, but when I fall,
I definitely rise and even crawl
To pen my rhymes and verses;
Regrettably, I didn't learn to fly
So my beloved winged horses
Ironically neigh passing me by.

Berserk

A mind directs a man.
A man is smaller than his mind.
A mind is a ceaseless universe.
A man is just a single verse…

I hear the heavy steps
Descending from the clouds,
I hear the echoes of my doubts,
I hear the tides debate the ebbs.

A psychologically inept persona
Is permanently set for a suicide;
Just like a virginal Madonna
That hadn't been a willing bride.

Conviction comes from an example;
Strongly persuading, vastly ample;
Even the chosen words don't work;
They are entirely eerie and berserk.

Earnings

My wife spent all my earnings
On jewelry and glitzy clothing;
She didn't care for other things;
In vain, she tried to learn to sing…

But after a week or two of practice,
She only learned to yelp and grate,
As if she ate a bitter thorny cactus
To constipate or lose some weight.

A Magic Wand

Men learned to speak...
The end of hide-and-seek:

A cradle of communication;
It was a magic wand,
That changed our lives,
We found our beehives...
A fragile, but eternal bond,
Peace over our frustration.

The dawn of our salvation...

Icing Soul

My rather advanced stage
Of a psychiatric crumbling
Delivered yet another page
Of my disjointed mumbling.

My world is just a total void:
There is no beam of light,
There is no pit of darkness,
There is no left or right…
Avoid!!!
Or live in the total starkness.

All of a sudden, a gentle light
Poked through a tight keyhole
Into my dark and dusty room;
A child who left a cozy womb,
To cross the friendless night,
And to caress my icing soul.

Sinai

Great Moses climbed that hill,
Looked at the burning bush,
Then heard the loud voice,
And got the Ten Commandments;
He knew it was our Savior's choice.

For some it still remains a paradigm
Of never-ending pull-and-push
Around failures and advancements.

For others it was a futile noise
And they don't give a dime.

Bigger

Great poetry is bigger than its writer,
It is convincingly audacious,
It is more vigorous; it is much brighter,
It is inviting, generous, and gracious…

It is the promised bread for our intellects,

Firstborn

A child is a true extraterrestrial creation;
No memories of pain, no good and evil…
The poison of our all-forgiving admiration
Shapes monsters with their brutal hearts,
And merciless, all-devouring minds;

Integrity and elegance are needless arts,
A daily lack of wisdom numbs and blinds.

I see you in pursuit:
I could have sworn,
You pulled the gun.
Don't start the strife,
Don't shoot!!!
I am firstborn,
I am your sun,
I am your life.

Spears

We exercise, we run through life,
We even try to get a little younger;
But neither I nor my beloved wife
Are engineers of our deep emotions;
We learned to fight our hunger
And float along the endless rivers,
We carefully cross the dicey oceans
Between the takers and the givers...

But at the bitter end,
We can no longer wait...
The spears of our fate
Pierce our hearts...
We see the Promised Land
To coexist by fits and starts.

Psychotic Prophets

We are psychotic prophets of our godforsaken lands,
We act like eager moppets in teachers' mighty hands.

We are conductors of ideas, mechanics of the minds,
We are presumptuous divas that blindly lead the blinds.

We fly above the sea of tears, between the fights and plays,
From a long comedy of years into a tragedy of happy days.

We turn the fortune's wheels against the legal blocks;
And learn the burning thrills behind the jailers' locks.

When autumn brings Orion into the unsuspicious skies,
Above the scorched horizon, above the fiery butterflies,
We watch a carnival of stars through prisons' iron bars.

Today, at least, I am free,
No more a hostage of my verse,
Today, I am a priest of glee
Just one of the church's whores.

Regrettably, I Lost …

My heartless empty chest looks like a phantom of a cage,
Or like a carcass of a ruined house;
My timid tombstone stands like a nasty symbol of despair.
The quitters do the very best, flaunting a pretentious rage;
I hear profanity-laced rants of every lucky second mouse,
A high-pitched noise I can no longer bear.

My life is a gigantic question without a necessary answer;
As the sad irony of my vocation, my views aren't innocent:
My sharp and entertaining language lets me swear,
Assembling the most attractive and intriguing scent.

A dark and murky yesterday fused with the bright tomorrows,
Delivers birth of a gloomy today draped in the quilt of sorrows.
I didn't choose to hibernate; my life is hanging on a hair:
I have to passionately wait for my foretold nightmare.

Fresh chill of winter snows and loud echoes of spring rains,
Forecasted autumns' golden glows and brutal hurricanes,
I sadly watched the hectic fall of my dog-tired yellow pages
Wearily but thoroughly remembering my life;
Then I received a luring call and jumped into the pit of ages.

Regrettably, I lost my final strife.

She is My Unwritten Page

Glee dwells in yesterdays, quite rarely in tomorrows,
Abandoning todays. The past appears as daily holidays,
The future as a joy without sorrows,
The present as the eternal maze.

I loved her hungry, luscious lips,
I loved her cheery, joyous mood,
Then why met the tinted horsemen of the apocalypse
Before my guarding angel knocked on wood?

Insomnia's alarming light casts demons on my soul.
Another sleepless night, another poisoned waterfall.

Even a lethargic sleep may end someday,
I learned to laugh, I learned to weep,
I learned to sin, but couldn't learn to pray.

My loneliness is horrid; I miss her on my page,
She isn't sad or worried, she simply left my cage.
She left that quiet nook without tears of outrage,
I am her unopened book, she is my unwritten page.

.

.

The Last Train Station

The last train station, I bought a one-way ticket
From earlier translation into the plain but wicked.

I won't be back,
I left this shore,
I run my own track,
Not a revolving door.

I am a sinner beyond help,
Beyond the thrown dice,
Beyond the primal word,
Beyond my bidding hand,
Beyond my hopeless yelp,
I see the Promised Land,
I see the bridges burned,
I see the ecstasy I earned,
I see the gate of paradise,
I see the sinless world…

I see no future at the end.

The Four

We hide from those Apocalyptic Four,
The red, the black, the pale, the white;
Yet we are searching for the other four,
For each inevitably God-given right:
Life, liberty, equality, and happiness,
But often wind up in a silent emptiness.

From dusk to down
There are no dramas and no thrills,
We are frustrated, bored and yawn,
Although, we have to pay our bills.

The wingless angels
Don't descend, they simply fall,
And dwell like fruitless strangers
In my tormented, grief-stricken soul.

Our ancient saints were worshiped
Years and years from dawn to dusk,
These days, their wings are clipped,
Their grandeur dwindling in the husk;
Our almighty man-created Lord,
We can no longer trust in you,
We are not standing in a queue
To hear from you the primal word.

We heard the deafening Big Bang,
We even heard the bells that rang;
They rang for you and me,
For all of those who were set free.

Iron Horse

My Ford, my iron horse,
Slow down, take it easy,
Look how many whores
Lined up and freezing…

Here is my basic plan,
I do this now and then:
I'll pick up the very best,
And leave alone the rest.
I'll tell her, please, turn off the key,
Sit still and wait; watch the police…
Immediately flee, before it is too late.

I'll lock the door, adjust the seat;
If nothing more, I'll like the treat;
She'll slowly bend; I've seen that show,
She'll give me hand, then kiss and blow.

She was quite cute,
She played my flute.

Heaven Can Wait

I drag like a heavy cross your love without a passion;
The amateurs and pros, the softness and aggression,
No one could wake you up to sip a nectar from a cup.
The passion of a starry night, the grandeur of a sunny day,
May bring you back in sight, although, you are so far away.

The pain of our farewells,
The first and happy date,
Play our melody on rails:
Heaven can wait,
Heaven can wait,
Heaven can wait...

I looked into your eyes; I touched your tender hand,
I heard your loving sighs; I held your wedding band.

You hid your face, my tiny nightingale,
Behind the silky lace of your bridal veil.

Your whitest dress,
Your sparkly eyes,
Our railroad tune;
The Orient express
Of virtues in the vice
Of our honeymoon.

Don't Try to Fly

Each is a useless organ: appendix, gut and brain;
No one would say a word on our abandoned train.
The passengers are gone, they left this timid world
On their exhausted feet to hear the godsend silence
Within the chill or heat; without our saints' guidance.

I am alone against the wall; farewell, red-hot Beirut,
You burned my weary soul; I kept my wartime loot:
A decorated wooden duck,
A photo of a lovely prostitute,
A head of a ten-pointer buck,
A good-luck rabbit foot.

If you are born to crawl, don't tease yourself,
Don't ever try to fly; it's not your downfall;
Just climb on your bookshelf,
And let a boredom pass you by.

Lives fly and whistle in the air
Like prehistoric arrowheads,
Between illusions and despair.

The Lord still pulls the threads.

Sieves

I read the know-everything tea leaves,
And press reality through many sieves.

Great women learn the art of aging,
Great actors never leave the stage;
My poems never flaunt their raging
Until I weave my final heartfelt page.

True poets don't predict our futures,
They are demanding to avert it.
For them tomorrows are already lit;
They see our wounds and sutures.

In high regard for archeology of death,
I searched the boneyards of the past:
The air was purer than a baby's breath,
The saddest banners moved half-mast.

Hell Lived in Me

I have received a magic spell
From one who never prays,
From one who rules this world,
A one who used to be the word.
For years, I lived quite well…
Hell lived in me those days…

Though, after he spent
Twelve moons with me,
He wouldn't talk to anyone:
To those who whined and bent,
To those who are afraid and flee,
To those who ran away and gone,
To those who are forever borrow,
To those who are quite often lent,
To those who drown in their sorrow,
To those who only steal and spend.

A physical defeat he turned into a moral victory for me:
I took a seat made from a rosy coral in his domain of glee.

The devil whispered something smart into my idle ear:
"Nobody dies from love; it is a mere poetic license
For those who met the Prince of Light but dwell in fear".

At dawn, the devil sows sparkly glares,
At dusk, we reap our happy love affairs.

Duration

Poetry is a bumpy road to somewhere,
It is a striking journey not a destination.
It is a search, it is a raid;
I must admit, I am afraid,
An aura of illusion is a tough backbone,
And yet, it is a shaky cornerstone
Of our salvation,
And possibly, of our infinite duration…

Homer, Flaubert, Tolstoy

Gustave Flaubert and Lev Tolstoy
Learned from the genius of Homer:
The critics are not fair; they destroy;
They want you as a trembling loner.

But you create,
You are the lightning rod;
In any rate, you are a god.

I keep the riffraff out,
I am laconic and decisive;
A real gods amnestied every doubt,
And pressed them through a sieve.

The stars are raining from the sky;
I am gone. Good luck. Goodbye.

Ballgame

The lifelong ballgame is still on:
The all-consuming flashy sounds
Have risen from the muddy grounds
To lull the looming stormy clouds,
To override uncertainty and doubts
And pitch them far-out-of-bounds.....

Under big riches often hides a crime;
The olden riches love this paradigm.

Choir

I wouldn't sing
In a church choir:
I am not a mourner,
I am not a teary crier,
I am just writing poems
In my tiny hole-and-corner.

There are no moral
Or immoral verses…
Just well or badly written, only…

The poets are, by nature, lonely.

Perfection

I never touched their wings,
I didn't rough their feathers,
I didn't steal their golden rings,
And other, so-called, treasures.

I sold my books under the sign
"Perfection Guarantied!"
I sold a lot,
I am doing fine;
They loved the read.

I bought a gorgeous yacht.
.

Cynic

Great cynic Nietzsche said:
Our God is dead!

What was the cause of death?
A heart attack, a colon cancer,
A disillusionment, a dire wrath
At our daily glee?

I am afraid, I know the answer:
It is too hard to be our God…

Please, pardon me,
There's a godsent lightning rod.

Prima Donna

The stream of her emotions
Runs like a waterfall of conscience
Into the lethargic, sleepy oceans
That are intangibly unconscious…

She runs into the cooler shades
From the intolerably scorching sun;
Just like the Queen of Spades
Toward the tempting twenty-one.

She leaves her age and ills behind,
She's our love; she's our prima donna,
She is so caring, generous and kind;
She is our godsent heaven's manna…

We are these crawling little ants;
She is the one who wears the pants.

Squeeze

A birch tree grows upside-down,
An old man wears a bridal gown,
Good learns to shoot and fight,
Evil becomes the blinding light.

I am still wearing my dog tag
Under the stripes of our flag.

I even try to squeeze
A single drop of tears
Out of my weary eyes;
A naughty morning breeze
Kicks in the teeth my fears…

I firmly rolled my farewell dice.

Bleacher

We love the paradigms:
The rooster crowed,
Peter three times
Betrayed his teacher;
Became a cornerstone
Of our tenuous beliefs.

Regardless qualms and ifs,
The seeds were sown
To put our souls' bleacher
High on the golden throne...
As glory to a godsent preacher.

Being an opium of the masses,
Faiths cover billions of asses.

Organism

A few regrettably forgotten parts
Of my ill-treated organism
Are rather wiser than their doctor.
My heart is knocking like a tractor;
My eyes enjoy the modern arts.
Muy artery is fighting an aneurism.

I miss my friends. I outlived them all;
I learned to fly. I wasn't born to crawl.

Stripped

The stage was whipped
By powerful projectors,
And we, the timid actors,
Unquestioningly stripped.

There is no present time,
Only a foggy mysticism;
There is no future time,
Only the sweet illusions.

There is our heavy past,
Our splendid classicism.

No More Bets

I wouldn't change the gears
Anticipating my fast demise;
The more intense the fears,
The longer stretch I agonize.

Neither have I joined all those
For whom a prison is a home;
Their freedoms decomposed
As changes in a metronome.

I am still waiting for the sun
After the moody red sunsets;
I want to see the mighty one
Who'll whisper: no more bets!

Lukewarm Sun

The nightly choreography of love
Between the hot but silky sheets
Was not enough...
Only the midday light
Exhausted our delight...
We went to get some eats.

I notice teardrops
Running from her eyes...
Time stops...
We wave our sad goodbyes.

The modest lukewarm sun
Cast trembling shadows,
Another noon has gone...

We Breed

We are alive; we breed;
At times, we even think.
Only the hearts of poets bleed;
We rhyme and write; it is our ink.

Religions almost died;
We, poets, are the teachers;
To substitute the preachers
Is not an easy ride...

Our pride is sliding downhill:
The ancient wars created heroes;
These days, only the rockets fight;
They badly wound and often kill,
But never create a single knight...

To Hear

These days, there are no cannonballs,
No castles with the moats and bridges,
No thick impenetrable walls,
No cavalry on sweaty horses...

These days, we climb the highest ridges
To hear the old confessions and remorses;
We resurrect the innocence of our youth
To hear and learn the real truth.

Schism

In vain, some dress their weakness
In the aggressive, violent sarcasm,
They try to show their uniqueness,
But it appears as a malicious spasm.

The real King of Nothing,
The punished angel,
The mighty Lucifer
Waving a gloomy banner
Of a never-ending void,
Of a baseless nihilism,
Of a malignant schism
That berthed those horrid four:
White, red then black and pale;
Conquest, Bloodshed then Famine
Inevitably trailed by Death.

I wonder who will catch my final breath.

Unaware

My very long and troubled life
Dealt with the absurdity of days
Like my continually irritable wife
Polishing the useless silver trays.

She always polished them at nights;
They couldn't reflect our daily fights.

We even argued whether or not the air
Remains a cause of our constipation,
Being entirely unashamed or unaware
Of our total intellectual castration.

We wanted a divorce;
Our minds, perhaps, may never heal:
The years of fighting left a sour taste;
It went from bad to worse:
The heartless judge denied our appeal.

I bet, we will forever coexist red-faced.

Posters

A life on roller-coasters,
I used to carry posters:

Bombing for peace
Is screwing for virginity!

Syphilis is a venereal disease
For fitness of The Holy Trinity!

A painless death
For a fresh breath!

Survived

My verses happily survived,
But cold as vodka in the freezer;
The reading public's pleaser
Must find the right time to thrive.

Poetry freely flows from me
Seamlessly rhymed,
Just like the artists' canvases
Already stretched and primed;
I only weave and type the strophes
Then as a hunter flaunt my trophies.

Morocco

A pair of unpredictable and lonely twins,
Two minarets entered the Southern sky.
Old constellations threw their blinking stars
Into the vulnerable, carefully climbing dawn;
I stop to write my self-indulging memoirs,
And like my quiet dog I stretch and yawn.

Gods pushed the darkness off the cliff;
My dog and I enjoy the raw tartar beef.

Daily Bread

We're not eating junk
For a few dollars less;
Only my wallet slightly shrunk
To tease our welcomed stress.

My girlfriend made a move
To stand and leave the table...
I knew she's willing,
She knew I'm able...

I lifted her and carried to my bed;
Long live forever our daily bread!!!

A Coin Has Been Flipped

Life's hopelessly opaque; I snoozed on its rock bottom,
You were a fragile snowflake who fell upon my autumn:
Our hearts were glowing, we madly fell in love
Without knowing who is a hawk, who is a dove.

Don't ever let me go away, I won't return.
I've read the script of this old-fashioned play.
A coin has been flipped. No roles to learn.
You chose the tails, I chose the heads,
You pushed the scales, I pulled the threads.

I lived a gender-bending life; you were unceasingly on top,
It was obnoxious penis-envy strife that wouldn't ever stop.

For this I paid a hefty price:
I am completely skinless,
I am unveiled and nude,
Alone, before your eyes:
I am a saint, I am sinless,
But I despise my solitude;

Although, I am not a thrall to power-hungry lenders,
I learned to veer and stroll along two equal genders.

A Fountain Without Water

My peerless fight held a muted sadness,
It stopped at night within a void of madness.
I didn't flip the silver quarter, but I was numb and strange,
I was a fountain without water; I was a bendy, leafless branch.

I was married to a grump through thick and thin,
I never played a trump; I had no chance to win.

My wings didn't unfurl,
I was perpetually wrong,
I never finished first,
I never caught that bird,
I never kissed that girl,
I never sang that song,
Too poorly versed,
I was a weary nerd.

I only loved my loyal dog from the beginning to the end,
A humble hero of my epilogue; my sweetheart, bosom friend.
Dawn brought a baby day wrapped up in laughter,
My dog and I found our highway to happiness forever after.

A glove

Another marriage fell apart
To justify our values' chart.

Each of the fates is blind
And tragically unneeded;
It is a fruit of a morbid mind,
Just like a victory conceded.

I marched my marriage trail,
I puffed the air of my defeat,
I could no longer bear the heat
From deadly toxins of betrayal.

Divorce was horrible, at best,
Just like a moth-eaten throw
That wrapped our dying love.

My wounded memory caressed
A farewell kiss she tried to blow
Without even taking off her glove.

The Heavy Clouds Hide the Stars

The house wins; no one to blame:
The never changing scene...
Every casino looks the same,
Even the tables are forever green.
So many songs haven't been sung,
So many verses are unwoven,
Too late to pray, the bell has rung,
My time is up; the dice were thrown.
The heavy clouds hide the stars,
My verse is dead, I see no muse,
My soul is locked behind the bars,
Above me not a halo, but a noose.

I live the final chapter of my book,
The happy end is never far away;
I never stirred my years; I shook;
The stars had shown me the way.

I know ills and I am not immune,
The healing melody is only one,
My soul is floating in that tune,

The farewell song of a dying swan.

Petrarchan sonnet

A vicious moth has eaten holes in my tuxedo,
These days, I can't afford to mend my suits,
These days, I deal with my diminishing libido,
My money left me through the chimney flutes.
I miss the hippie days of our psychedelic past,
I didn't like Chopin and kept him in the locker,
When quiet hours would never move too fast,
I loved The Beatles, Hendrix and Joe Cocker.

I thought it was a new Big Bang
When Eric Carmen fondly sang:
"And making love was just for fun,
Those days have gone…"
The melody of life has no refrain,
No words, only the strings of rain.

Adviser

It's never too late
To get a little wiser:
Life teaches us to hate,
Time is a great adviser.

The Bible said:
An eye for an eye,
A tooth for a tooth…
I'd like to add:
Dream of the sky,
But love the truth…

Artesian Well

Ascending to the mountaintops, a blustery and rubicund sunrise
Delivers sorrows and teardrops: two bitter dishes for a bulky price.

I asked my buttoned-down brain to share some thoughts with me,
The answer was, "I am insane; you have to ask the Wisdom Tree."

My rather acquiescent state of mind
Kindly allows perilous ideas to erupt,
I am frequently and fervently inclined
To act as if I am unspeakably corrupt.

The creek of daily skepticism fondles the skinless fairness
Of my disgruntled life of pain,
Leaving my childish nihilism with a discriminating sense
Of breathing proudly, in vain.

I sink into a persistent ocean of illusions,
I am drinking the murky waters of denial.
I am enduring some miracle transfusions
From a lethargic muddy swamp into a vial.

I put one foot affront the other far from my troubled childhood
Of promises to my controlling father who picks the ugly, not
the good.
I sleuth my way out of Hell; I am in the pursuit of bliss, I am a hound,
I am looking for my own artesian well with Holy water skyward
bound.

Begone

If our world's a glass half-empty
Why does it look like a half-full?
If our world is the Horn of Plenty
Am I the only living hungry fool?

I have no roles in modern plays,
I didn't learn the rules of games.

What do you do when you're away?
Where do I walk on my legs of clay?
I walk the stairway
To heaven; not very far away...

Let days begone
Remain begone...
I wouldn't blame the past,
I'm finally not there, at last.

Bellwether

I was a bellwether
Of a life unknown;
We laughed together,
But always cried alone.

Goodbye,
It's hard to be alone at night,
Goodbye,
It took a single beam of light
To bring a lovely baby-dawn;
I pulled my old guitar;
The darkness of a corner
Has quickly gone…

I sang: "The heaven isn't far,
But don't be yet a mourner,
Goodbye is not farewell;
It means I'll see you later,
But first, I'll descend to hell
Then I'll ascend to my creator."

Brutus

Man to man is wolf! Homo humini lupus!
The proof is Caesar's: "You too, Brutus!"

I am not fooled by glasses, masks, and wigs;
The more I know men, the more I like the pigs.

Chimera

We are living in the era
Of loneliness and doubts
Created by a fiery chimera
Wrapped in the stormy clouds.

The winged horse Pegasus,
My muse and is a noble steed.
We both are bold and generous,
But never surrender or concede…

We are flying thru the Milky Way
Above the chock-full sweaty bus
Packed with the critics hating us;
The jolly stars are kindly blinking;

This is my heavy drinking,
This is a freely writing day.

Coexistence

They chewed the fat of a small talk
Commonly laced with ambiguities;
I eagerly high-fived those deities,
And left behind their castigations;
It was my cunning diplomatic walk,
Possibly, fitting the United Nations...

Bland and unimaginative people
Try to imitate lobsters in a bucket:
When someone makes a ripple,
They pull him in a box and lock it.

Coexistence is a half-baked strife
Of typically two ravens with a hawk:
They vigorously cruise and croak,
But genially crave a noiseless life.

They are chaotic and disoriented;
We are the same. My story ended.

Cooing

The sun is hanging on my wall,
Two pigeons cooing on a window,
A day found a parking on my floor,
I heard a quiet knocking on my door,
Just like a gentle one hand clapping.
I finally woke up; enough of napping.

I am eager to confess:
I am afraid of nothing,
I fear no one. Nevertheless,
I picked my loaded gun,
Because I doubt everything
From dusk to dawn...

It was the only known truth,
It was the innocence of youth.

My complicated life became too fast,
Even my car appears unmoving;
I am writing and inching ahead, at last;

My nasty critics read and disapproving.

Deck

The sticks of Eastern hieroglyphs
Snappishly falling from the cliffs,
The olden knowledge disappears
Behind the walls of lies and fears.

A few pale stars still blink about,
The crescent went to sleep
Under a heavy rainy cloud,
The willows have begun to weep.

The sun will also rise.
Am I in paradise?

I've been into the belly of the beast,
I know how to avoid another wreck,
I need no sugar and no yeast,
I also rise; I keep all hands on deck.

Deja vu

I didn't have a clue
What we were fighting for,
I only knew my wounds and scars...
They were so-called the spoils of war;
They were free gifts of a bloody Mars.

Much later, a goddess Nike welcomed us
To breathe the dust behind a leaving bus.

Wars rarely used me as a vibrator
In their unending extramarital affairs;
Wars always used me as a gladiator
To fight and win and circle edgy squares.

Today, I strolled under the frozen skies,
Under the cotton clouds wrapped in ice,
I passed the taped up gates of paradise;
It's Déjà vu; I've been here once or twice

Devious

First ninety years
Of my tormented life:
No living friends or peers,
Some worries, but no fear

Perhaps in vein, life tied to unify
My wobbly body with my troubled soul;
By change, through a petite keyhole
I saw the truth: a trivial hogwash knee-high.

My gifted daily life
Is just a skillful midwife
Delivering the cutest baby-dawns
Made not from real gold but bronze.

There is nothing more devious
Than so-called forthright facts
Creating myths and legendary heroes
Neglecting oaths and signed contracts.

Although, these days, my life aligned
With youth that didn't know war or hunger;
The young are endlessly talented but blind
Until they face betrayals, lies and anger...

Devotion

The noose of literary critics
Demonically descending from above...

For my sadistic, merciless pseudo analytics
It is the true manifestation of their real love,
And their devotion to murdering my rhymes,
But fortunately, not always. Just sometimes.

Discouraged

I am standing at the very end
Of a discouraged lifelong line;
It's not an up-to-the-minute trend:
At times, life is the thinnest twine,
Sometimes, it is the thickest rope
That suffocates my fragile hope…

I am waiting for the amnesty from God,
His Son erased my sins but not enough,
Regrettably, only a ruthless firing squad
May finish our sins and reestablish love.

Discourse

You came as spring into my life,
I knelt and you become my wife.

Just like a deafening ovation,
Just like a cascade of celebration,
Just like a blinding light of a sunrise
Reflected in your always happy eyes.

You left right in the middle of discourse
Between the better and the worse...

Distant Sadness

As long as I shall live
I'll be standing at the cliff
Dividing good and bad,
Dividing hungry
And their daily bread…
I am alive and I am angry.

Some losers are remembered,
Some heroes-winners we forget,
Their legends are dismembered,
But we the butchers don't regret.

I used to strike all-in-one words
Long nights from dusk to dawn,
Creating yet unknown worlds…
Those wonder days long gone.

Nostalgia is not a joy,
Nostalgia is a distrait sadness,
Nostalgia is not a charming toy,
Nostalgia is a sheer madness.

Dozen

It is so late, a day already slumbers;
I read the weirdest book of numbers:

We vibrantly remember our first love,
We run a course on a second breath,
We know the gifts of three wise men,
We try to touch the fourth dimension,
We search for a fifth corner in a room,
We cultivate and use our six senses,
We veer alongside seven deadly sins,
We possibly prefer eight days a week,
We never shop in a local nine-eleven,
We accidently missed the perfect ten;
We cruised to twelve-the lucky dozen.

I asked my friends,
Am I the first to love a second cousin?
The history repeats but never ends...

Essence

Time is of the essence
In my chess game for life
Delays never make any sense
In this rather unexpected strife.

I must return after a violin
Will end its teary farewell;
I'll stop my churches' bell;
To let my death enjoy the win.

Ever

Don't sing this song to anyone,
This song is just for you and me;
It is about our ever rising sun,
It is about our never-ending glee.

I sieved the myriads of words
To find a few morsels,
To write the finest rhymes of life,
As sharp as the ancient swords.

I placed them in the midst of strife
Between the good and evil forces.

They reached the highest roof,
Nobody ever window-shopped,
The elevator stopped…
They all got off together
Into the infinitely rainproof,
The true divinity of sunny weather.

Fleeced

I lived and crawled along my rhythmic lines
Toward a thrilling sense of urgency to write
Without any faith, without any warning signs;
Their silhouettes just whispered in a distance
Something about good and evil, day and night,
Something about values of friendly coexistence.

Hello, cabby, give me a lift,
Please, take me to my priest;
Let me return his useless gift
Of my religion. I was fleeced.

From Afar

For almost ninety years
I floated on the current
With human odds and ends;
I thought they were my peers,
I thought they were my friends;
They definitely weren't.

I write, I never miss a day:
About just a single star
Of our endless Milky Way
That guides me from afar.

I am trying to invite my readers
To plunge into the grumpy oceans
Of our intellectual sensations:
Far from the lazy bottom feeders,
Into the depth of genuine emotions
Deserving our exuberant ovations.

Fruitless

I told my fruitless hope,
Get off me to the ramp;
Fate sealed my envelope,
And even glued the stamp.

I did invite y'all to my table,
Bring a true story or a fancy fable,
Bring me your hunger, pain and thirst;
You're not the last, you're not the first.

You did alienate your relatives,
You did estrange your friends:
Your lives are full of negatives...

I do anticipate the happy ends.

Godsend

The sun lit edges of the clouds,
Dismissing the night of doubts;
I haven't seen such beauty since
I stopped enjoying my easy wins.

The dying golden autumn leaves
Are curling down to my shoulders,
As a reminder of my deepest griefs
Eternal as the Sisyphus boulders…

I heard: "Don't blame your life
If you can't stand the heat…
Just try to win this lifelong strife;
It is a godsend most delicious treat!"

Graffiti

Please, take a shower.
It's not a time for glory;
Don't throw in the towel,
I'm here to tell the story.

The tired snow melts
It is the rite of spring,
The time to tighten our belts
And take a lazy morning stroll;
The birds don't sing,
I read graffiti on the wall:
"Unjustly written law
Is like a rough chainsaw;
Not every problem is a nail,
Not every solution is a hammer.
We fail to trust,
We choose to bail,
A jail is not a must,
Unlock the slammer."

The jailed birds will never sing
Not even for the rite of spring.

Grosser

Our passed relatives awakened...
Each got what he or she deserves,
High-spirited and cheerfully naked,
Wrapped in my comfortable verse,
And ready for a better second life...
I looked a little closer:
Oh, no! It was my second wife...
Life has become a little grosser.

Hell Lived in Me

I have received a magic spell
From one who never prays,
From one who rules this world,
A one who used to be the word.
For years, I lived quite well…
Hell lived in me those days…

Though, after he spent
Twelve moons with me,
He wouldn't talk to anyone:
To those who whined and bent,
To those who are afraid and flee,
To those who ran away and gone,
To those who are forever borrow,
To those who are quite often lent,
To those who drown in their sorrow,
To those who only steal and spend.

A physical defeat he turned into a moral victory for me:
I took a seat made from a rosy coral in his domain of glee.

The devil whispered something smart into my idle ear:
"Nobody dies from love; it is a mere poetic license
For those who met the Prince of Light but dwell in fear".

At dawn, the devil sows sparkly glares,
At dusk, we reap our happy love affairs.

Hold On

Hold on to hopes; keep them alive;
Don't be a bee that lost her hive…

My guiding angel isn't fair,
He doesn't have the wings;
There is no end to my despair,
The tireless evil pulls my strings;
I am his well-trained marionette:
He swims in gains; I sink in debt.

I sunk my teeth into my guilt
And couldn't see a thing around,
Although, my eyes are pilled,
To watch my horse's final round…

In any case,
It was the glimpse of glee:
We won that crucial race,
And those who trusted me
Were happy at the cashier's window,
Loading their pockets with the dough.

Hold or Fold

Even in the darkest nights
I am looking for the lights,
Often in vain;
Wisdom is bursting from my phone
To entertain my pain.

It says: truth must be told...
Nobody knows whether to hold or fold
Even the darkest story
Deserves the lights of godsend glory.

Youth has to be exuberant and stupid,
The wise recollect their bitter sorrows,
A young man is just a wingless cupid,
The old man always fears tomorrows.

The modern cult of careless youth
Is just a mindless journey of the blind:
They are afraid of the unknown truth,
No one may even recognize their find.

Holiness

It was the end of our affair,
I heard her sweet goodbye;
Life drank the wine of my despair,
Life played its nasty, vicious role,
Life didn't try to buy,
I didn't dare to sell my soul…

I loved my loneliness,
My oneness with the world;
I loved my unpredicted Holiness:
I was the one who knew the word.

Horizon

We calm our souls
And chain our hearts
To looming nonexistent walls,
Just to be pierced by cupid's darts.

I hear your sighs,
You know I am near;
You fight a sticky fear
Of love that often stops;
I kissed two small teardrops
In corners of your saddest eyes.

We play charades across the fences;
Red sunset fades; Gene Kelly dances
In the eternal rain; white seagulls dive
Into the sea of pain; into the ending life.

The gray horizon hangs along the bluff,
We navigate among our foes and friends,
Nike unfurled her wings above our love,
Bad movies always get the happy ends.

Husk

Above the sunlit gables
The sky's blue ceiling
Creates a gentle feeling
Of children's quiet fables.

The golden dress of maples
Swirls into the winter's freeze,
Into the calm of a vowed bliss,
Into the anxious flow of fables.

I run from a chilling dusk
Toward an inviting dawn;
I crave to peel the husk
Off the unknown paragon.
I want to turn it on a dime
Into a balanced paradigm.

I Hear the Drums of War

Despair is near; I hear the angry drums of war,
But crafty and insincere like kisses of a whore.

The songs of our sons
Sung by the fallen stars
After the quiet dawns,
Before the loud guns.

I hate the melodies of flying missiles
They freeze my will, they irritate my ears.
Wars have no remedies to calm those whistles,
Even the victories don't cure our constant fears.

Caress your scars,
They are still sore,
The dice are thrown;
The wars will never end,
Enjoy your girls and bars,
Until we start another war:
The end of wars is known
Only to the dead.

I Never Count Chickens

I never count chickens before they hatch;
Till autumn thickens, I never lift the latch.

I realized that I was blind then morphed into a normal fool;
I grabbed and threw my mind into a life-devouring whirlpool.

Nostalgia runs pictures of a past; I saw that movie many times;
I watched my scars forever last as punishments without crimes.
I marched with mop-and-bucket toward the tunnel's lighter end;
Time passed; I simply ducked it, until God asks me to ascend.

I heard a growing drumbeat of the ancient actors' final days;
It is the time to take the heat; I am leaving the modern plays;
I am stepping off the stage; my teapot whistles its head off,
My parrot's cursing in his cage. I left my lifetime cozy trough.

I still have a few hours to pack my old tuxedo for the parting ball;
My best foot touched the track; I heard the fat lady's curtain call.

Nobody Heard the Word

Nobody heard the word
Which started our world.

A word is just a piping bird,
She is gone; she is away;
Before we heard the word,
Before we went to pray.

She flies beyond the seas
To find what we've lost.
Don't change the diocese
The Lord is our new host.

A word is just a word,
What's in the name?

Farewell, my friend,
A bird is in my hand.
If this is our world
Who is to blame?

I Never Knew My Saints

I never knew my saints, I always knew the sinners,
My memory of losers fades, I don't forget the winners.

I notice, when I stare, we are all equal if we are naked,
Our souls ascending bare; it is the fact; I didn't make it.

About forty years must pass, before we judge our heroes.
Sobriety descends on us, we see ourselves in dirty mirrors.

Our foreverness
Is straight ahead emerges as a godsend blast;
Nevertheless,
I break my daily bread with friends who passed.

I hardly see the signs
Of love and hate, delights, and sorrows;
But I can see the lines
Of those who wait for infinite tomorrows.

I Overshot the Runway

Under the total moon eclipse from early dusk to dawn,
Four Horses of Apocalypse just trotted and were gone.
They plunged to the abyss of waterless forsaken wells,
Taking the gold of maple trees to places no one dwells.
Don't wait for the next eclipse; you'll miss the wedding bells;
Don't hide your honey lips, the pricey pearls inside the shells.

I knelt; looked in your eyes
And bravely threw the dice:
You're my altruistic spring
Wrapped in a silky blanket;
Here is your diamond ring…
I prearranged the banquet.

Another knot is tied,
Another starry night,
Another tight embrace,
Another golden cage,
The key is laid aside;
As old as the hills,
Another apple's bite,
I kissed her baby-face:
Old book— new page,
The same old thrills.

I overshot the runway; the world became insane:
The trees won't sway; my love has failed in vain.

I Reaped a Hurricane

I sowed the wind,
I reaped the hurricane;
I lived, I loved, I sinned:
God's loss; the devil's gain.

I drift between the souls,
I am a boat without sails,
I lost my aims and goals,
I am a train without rails.

In the periphery of life,
I am at least the second best;
I flaunt my victories and thrive,
And seldom lose like all the rest.

It is the valor of a foolish child,
But I am in the pursuit of fights,
I am rogue and absolutely wild,
Often alone against the tides

My life is fauna wrapped in flora,
A tiny bit of ecstasy in every day,
But I am ready for a kind tomorrow,
I am climbing the celestial stairway.

Isolated

I am feeling isolated
In crowds of my peers;
In spite of similar and mostly fated,
The aura of upbringing disappears.

Even the tender innocence of youth
Will go under the decomposing truth.

I try to keep four tires on the wheels,
Though, our world remains Jurassic;
It hardly ever wonders stray
From its inherited barbarity;
Its failed traditions became classic
And now hesitantly pass away…

I am feeling isolated from my peers…

La Petit Mort

We went through every little death,
La petit mort as they say in French,
Of our exciting carnal knowledge;
It was the most exhilarating path
Through our lovemaking college
In which nobody loses. No revenge.

I worked my way
To a position on my back;
The second phase of our play…
Just like a midday snack,
A cup of coffee and a gulp of air.
She calls the shots. I humbly dare.

But if I fail, I'd pet my loyal dog…
She has to kiss that horrid frog…

Latched

I lived and made a few mistakes;
I took some puddles for the lakes:
I met some undeserving people,
Each dropped and made a ripple.

I always keep my fingertips
On a weak pulse of masses;
Meanwhile my conscience slips
Under the downtown overpasses.

I've read the morsels of tealeaves,
Almost erased yet still attached
To my well-known past,
But couldn't show my tomorrows
As if some grieving thieves
Deliberately and firmly latched
Sweet dreams and bitter sorrows
Of my illusions that forever passed.

Life Left a Lipstick Mark

Rainfalls morph into snowstorms; it is a rollercoaster ride
Along the unexpected turns between humility and pride.
I am a reluctant debutant; I am still treading icy waters,
I am a lofty aspirant; I try to foil guillotines from slaughters.

Our emotions stopped in unison
And breathed until no one is left,
Even the fallen angels mourn
This human cataclysmic theft.

Well done above well said,
I am a gawking, wrathful lad
Demolishing this nonsense and cruelty of these clichés.
I'm a rhymester with license to R.I.P. on Pere Lachaise;
Pardon my jumbled French.
My oddly enigmatic fantasy is rather flawlessly sincere:
I carved it on a hoary bench,
A simple evangelic fallacy: "Mon Vie Est Mon Plaisir!"
The earthly daily splendor Is a strategic sleeping bag,
I'll never ever wave the flag of unconditional surrender.

I am like a jovial lark in glee up to my beak,
Life left a lipstick mark on my unshaven cheek.

Math

Her easy-to-follow calculation
Was just a basic first-grade math,
And yet, her well-asphalted path
Led me into a devout admiration.

She kept her hair uncombed,
But always fresh and airy;
First date: I was forever stunned
By splendor of that sweet cherry.

She was a little on a plump side,
I noted when I took her for a ride;
She wore a see-through negligee;
Good starter, but greater as entre.

I jammed my foot into the door,
In premonition of a civil war;
It hardly ever pays to be polite
Before the domination fight...

We are still fighting in the trenches
Instead of kissing on the benches
Or holding hands in our cozy park.

It looks as if a wolf has met a shark.

Matthew

The crown of thorns,
The passion, the true cross,
A triumph of a godsent loss:
The world still mourns...

I often read the gospel
According to St. Matthew:
It seems to me forever new;
Just like a highway hostel
On our path into the light...

Keep reading; I will write.

Medium Rare

Love broke my heart; the ancient unforgotten art.
I pushed banalities aside; my innocence has died.

My soul is lying bare; the merciless sunrays jeer it.
I ordered medium rare; so the abyss won't sear it.
I heard, our faded souls rest in the city of the dead,
Without dreams, without goals, without daily bread.

I've read on the title page: we're all actors, life is a stage;
The play has ended: we are free to burn our wisdom tree.

In quest for our universal paradigm
The mavens never used their heads;
They tried to save their fruitless time,
And jerked the actors with the threads.

There's no cooler side on my creased pillow,
Only a sleepless mind, only a weeping willow
Instead of the Garden of Eden wisdom tree…

And neither we are free.

Microwave

Death was the primal word,
Forgotten even by the Lord…

I took a comfortable seat
Whichever one is closest to my grave;
A stone's-throw away
From my coffin and its final microwave.

The fiery abyss is always lit
And I am timely on the way.

My weary and unshaven soul
Mercilessly condemned to die,
Waiting blindfolded at the wall,
And has no time to learn to fly.

I don't have anything
To prove to anyone…
I want only a single thing:
To see a one more dawn.

Mirrored

Our creation in His own image
Wasn't the tired Lord's mistake:
Regrettably, He had a dire day;
Maybe it was a daily scrimmage
Between the even give-and-take
Somewhere along the Milky Way.

The stars were mirrored in the seas,
Our souls completed their striptease.

Morsels

My relevance is undisputed;
I write, somebody always reads;
Only my critics, being too stupid,
Destroy the sowed by me seeds.

In premonition of the red sunset,
That horrid messenger of Mars,
The mean ambassador of threat
To my beloved stars-and-bars,
Has reaffirmed my motto-mission:
Don't ever lie to our young,
Don't poison our tomorrows…
Their songs may die unsung…
And drown in the seas of sorrows.

My limericks and parables,
My deeply heartfelt verses,
At times, are mighty pearls,
At times, are futile rubbles,
But studded with the morsels
After the vigorous rehearsals.

My Autumns Were Your Springs

My autumns were your springs,
You let me spread my wings;
You were so innocently young,
You were a song but yet unsung.

The eagle of that love still flies,
High in the ocean of the skies.

We used to soar together,
Two restless, troubled souls,
Two birds; different feathers;
Two radicals, different goals.

We climbed too high,
We burned our wings;
The sun's apologetic sigh
Fell from its blinding rings.

Our happy careless hearts
Pierced by the cupid's darts,
Dismissed the warning bell,
We touched the sun. We fell.

My Blue-Eyed Pond

My blue-eyed pond, you are my muse,
My happy wand, my devastating blues.
Compassion rules the world stirred by our trusting hearts,
By problems of the world reflected in the obscurity of arts.

Until my thoughts deserted me forever,
Until the clockwork of my weary heart
Stopped making its mystifying noises,
I tore apart the hair thin lifelong thread
That braiding me with fates and faiths,
Dreams, hopes and laughs of people;
My fingertips felt their lackluster pulse,
My ears heard words of the beginning,
I viewed my angels in the thick of night,
I ran and fell before I climbed the wall,
I saw the burning bridge of yesterdays.
And saw a quiet death of my own past.

I'll cross the street; I'll walk the sunny side;
I'll tolerate the heat; I'll learn to run and hide.
I'll stretch my mind; I'll need a cozy shade;
I'll swallow vanity and pride; I'll leave the stage and fade.
I'll have no one to blame; I'll withdraw from this game;
I'll erase my tarnished name from the quagmire of fame.
I'll leave my soul; I'll sell my flesh,
I'll fall and crawl; I'll take the cash.
I'll never reach the clouds; I'll never touch the stars;
I'll be lonely in the crowds; I'll dwell behind the bars.
I'll part the gloom from the fanfare; I'll reach the pits of the abyss,
I'll seek the darkness of despair and only then, I'll ascend to bliss.

Necromancer

I am always vigilant, attentive;
At times, I am quite inventive...

I wrote a letter to the Lord,
I asked for our primal word.

My angel said:
"Your wish is granted,
I sealed the envelope
And stamped it;
He'll read. Let's hope,
It will be answered..."

I am ninety, still waiting
For a one word answer
But daily pray, the Lord
Is not a necromancer...

Nirvana

My spacious glassy hall
Lit by the gleaming moon,
The Mona Lisa on the wall,
Forged by a native goon.

A glass of a red wine
Between two candles,
The night erased a line
Between two genders…

A tenor sings a serenade
To his beloved concubine,
The gloomy shadows fade,
I drown my luscious wine.

Nirvana covers me with silk,
Pure as my mother's lullaby,
The lazy stars forgot to blink,
I whisper to my worries, bye.

No Chastity in Me

The gods divided our glee…
There are two equal parts:
Some sided with reality
I sided with the arts.

I looked for the elusive gene; I ripped apart my DNA,
I split morality from its hygiene, there is no other way.

I've seen the Prince of Light;
Jerusalem, Palm Sunday night:
Red carpets faded, the palm trees wilted,
The history was raided, the truth was tilted.

Then gentle dawn morphed into a sunny day.
I acted as a faun; a monster on feet of clay
I rang the bell until it melted under the brutal sun.
My faith was dented in that malicious hit-and-run.

Don't look for chastity in me,
I am not a saint, I am not entirely pure.
Gods didn't make my honesty carefree;
They disappeared but didn't leave the cure.

No More

My critics try to jail and execute
My creativity and then myself…
No more lackluster off-the-shelf
Is a heroic moto of my pursuit.

A mother of my verse is music,
A father of my poetry is grief…

A word is a fallen golden leaf.

Is this a time to wish and hope?
Is this a time for great illusions?
Is this a time for my conclusions?

This is a time to noose the rope!

Odd

The ripples from my dreams
Still rock my fragile hopes;
My muddled future screams,
Please, never noose the ropes!

I visit my future from time to time,
She sleeps beneath the sod...
The boneyard's strident paradigm
Seems very unemotional and odd.

Painkillers

Painkillers never cure our ills,
Or any other slick, but futile pills;
The fallen angel comes and kills.
We only pay our enormous bills.

The prisms of my imagination
Divided daily streams of life
In seven colors and seven days;
The train of doubts left the station,
I had divorced another lovely wife.

Life runs, but my exhaustion stays.

My eyes are dusty mirrors…
They saw the past and our heroes,
But can't predict tomorrows,
That even the Lord unlikely knows.

Paranoid

The lasting truths are still naïve,
They're not familiar with infinity,
Only the lies have lost virginity,
Admiring their earliest lady Eve.

Sometimes, I am acutely clever,
I often leave just for a minute,
But wave my farewells forever;
My friends are shocked and mute;
They think I am severely paranoid,
But I am just annoyed: I see a void.

I can foresee another war:
A highly profitable business,
But mother, don't invest your son:
He'll never see another Christmas,
By winter, he'll be forever gone…

Our good wishes cannot stop the wars;
Life is a sinking boat; no sails and oars.

Pebbles

Time never heals,
It never moves,
It has no wheels,
It has the devil's hooves.

"Good time is not what you deserve",
I've heard it from my heartless boss;
"I eat and drink; you only serve";
I shut the door; hot as a chili souse.

I walk along my dream
With pebbles in my shoes;
Sometimes I laugh,
But often sing the blues;
My life is not a heavy cream,
It's just a half-and-half...

Philosophy

Life starts with a baby's breath,
Life ends with the fear of death.

Philosophy is a coquetry of thoughts,
It is a cacophony of nervous throats,
It is an ineffective intellectual flirtation,
It is a fictional train that left the station.

It has no written rules, no burdens,
It pulls apart the heavy dusty curtains,
And lets us see the real truth,
Even the lightness of our being,
Even a shameless innocence of youth,
The every so often sad ability if seeing.

Pigsties

As a descendent of the pilgrims,
I dump on you my crazy whims:

My beyond doubt troubled life
Is like a rickety peace treaty:
It only roars from eight to five,
Like urban wisdom of graffiti.

I killed a bonfire in my soul
With a few swigs of whisky,
But missed my noble goal,
It was too unsafe and risky:
I aimed to lock all humans-
The real devils in disguise,
In our muddiest pigsties
And free the grieving pigs
From those unsanitary digs.

I often mutter in my gigs:
The more I know people,
The more I like the pigs.

Piles

The rays of sun never descend
On the green brightest tables,
The gamblers like the horses
Who never leave their stables,
And hope to avoid the bitter end.

The betting engineered my mind,
The greed left everything behind.

We supplement a dame of pique
With gallantry of ace of hearts,
And hope to win the piles of cash;
We play a game of hide-and-seek
Under the flying Venus' darts,
Piercing the innocence of our flesh.

Pneumonia

Each early dawn
Gives us a day unknown,
Desirable and valuable,
Its fee is highly overblown...

A whisper of long frozen twigs
Caressed a fender of my car...
They were the same old pigs
As every human near and far.

One of them slowly walked,
She had pale skin, red lips,
Gray hair and brown eyes...
The fragile late winter ice
Untimely, traitorously cracked,
A woman gone under the water;
I was too drunk to start a motor.

I quickly dived and pulled her out;
She got pneumonia and later died.
Oh, well... at least, I tried.

Pursuit

The most exciting part of any hunt
Is the emotional and skilled pursuit;
Although, it may be long and blunt;
While you remain completely mute.

The early sun caressed the pond,
A few unlucky ducks
Disturbed the sleepy silence…
I aimed and pulled the trigger twice.
My black retriever brought two birds,
And earned his yummy treat…
Our bond defined by Pavlov's science
Puts thrilling dinners on my table…
He's always willing and I'm quite able.

Raft

I face a raft of challenges,
My self-reliance crumbles,
And even when I'm playing chess,
My Queen continuously stumbles.

A dreaded fallen angel
Appeared once more,
Just like the night before,
Treading with mighty steps
As if he is not a stranger
But came to pay his debts.

Life is a cruel barfly; she is a whore,
She keeps me off her moving bus;
That is a pronouncement of a war,
I have to use my powers en masse.

Regularly

We're all wounded, never healed
By our love affairs or lack of them;
Love is a bloody battlefield,
But hardly is a precious gem...

Love is so sweet and so attractive,
Sometimes, even its failure is a joy...
Love is like the sleepy horse of Troy,
Only at night it is belligerently active.

Our anger constantly diverts us
From what we call a happy living;
We regularly bite the dust
Behind the moving bus of being...

Rusts and Moths

The rusts and moths
Destroyed my treasures,
But left the truth without clothes:
My youth's forgotten pleasures.

Exit

The Mass was foggy and uncertain.
Here is a scene behind the curtain...

I told my minister:
"In more than twenty timid years
I heard all your redundant stories,
Always unclear and even sinister...

My dreams had died without glories
Boding my disillusionment and exit
From this assumed to be His house...

But I am the lucky second mouse".

Fascination

My morbid fascination with the past,
And premonition of the atomic blast,
Morphed me into a cynic with no fear:
I tell the people what they hate to hear.

A very few of us enjoyed the past:
Confusing, woozy and half-assed.

Some chose self-beatings,
The others liked their cries;
I truly loved the greetings,
No farewells, no goodbyes,
No footprints of my age.

I didn't write my final page.

Schmoozer

Perhaps my wartime childhood
Made me a much better writer,
And led me out of the flaming wood
That didn't need a half-baked critic,
A literary know-it-all chronic paralytic,
But rather a brave expert firefighter.

I had devoured myriads of books
For breakfast, lunch and dinner...
The jocks assumed I was a loser;
But I became a wayward poet-winner,
And for the parties a great schmoozer.

I never liked a goodbye kiss,
The sign of a delight that passed;
I would prefer infinity of bliss,
Or something worthy of a quiet rest...

Scream

The lightning split the sky between the shaky stars;
The fields were almost dry along the tractor's scars.
The winds formed ripples in quiet waters of the lake;
A such a pleasant treat; a ripen cherry on the cake.

I changed the horses in my life's midstream;
I burned my early verses to hear their scream
Under the leaky roof of shredded clouds,
Above my heroes resting in their shrouds.

Life killed my innocence, time crashed my youth;
I learned to recognize only a meek axiomatic truth.

I watched a human shark caught in the mousetrap;
I saw the bridge connecting us was quickly burned,
It was the earliest Rubicon still shining in the dark;
The seas consumed the choke-packed Noah's ark;

Autonomy to start new wars was promptly earned…

Sfumato

I trust it is my inborn moto:
Life is a cloudy sfumato;
Thus fear no one and nothing,
But dare to doubt everything.

God usually saves only those
Who tried to save themselves;
Bliss is a stone throw distance;
My stairway of least resistance
Is a lackluster wingless prose
I write and hide on dusty shelves.

Life piled me with too many questions,
But I am not prepared to take the blame;
My answers are more or less the same:
Rapid rejections offered as suggestions.

She was so Young and Fresh

She was so young and fresh,
Even her knees were scratched;
A tender flower in flawless flesh
Her eyes and heavens matched.

Against her charm and beauty
There was no valuable defense.
She was nineteen, a real cutie;
Alone. First time in France…

I ate her with the spoon,
I dived into my youth again…
I was a wild and hungry goon;
Nothing to lose. Only to gain.

The merciless sound of alarm
Was loud as a cow on the farm;
When I woke up, I sadly wept,
It was my wettest dream. I slept.

She Wasn't There

There's no free lunch, even in France:
I asked: how much for love after this dance?

I love Parisian hookers,
Their pimps, their bookers
Working on Rue Saint-Denis:
The heaven of my nightly glee.

"Don't tell me c'est la guerre:
It is a war, life is unfair;
Don't offer me ménage a trios
It isn't yet my last hurrah;
Just come to bed."
"I love you, too", she said.

But when I woke, she wasn't there,
I rolled and lit a smoke; I was a lonely hare.

At noon, she has returned,
She looked directly in my eyes:
"I am entirely booked; it is my paradise;
Go back to bed; so long; I work the Gars,
In France, your lovely stars and bars
Are yet unfurled."

Short Summer Rain

Short summer rain, long lazy stream,
The strands of pain poured to the rim.

A worthless flight,
The weary shrouds hover my dreams,
Another pretty sight
Between the clouds, along the beams.

I am cold,
The tired sun can't warm me anymore.
No time to fold
Before the storm, before another war.

My wisdom wasn't cheap,
I dearly paid for every tiny bit
Of this sacramental leap;
The gate to heaven wasn't lit.

I burned a sky-high pile
Of wishes and desires,
Ignited by my smile
And vanities' bonfires.

Sincerely

In youth, I drank my friends
Under the table;
In youth,
I was a real hero for the girls,
But even then, I have been able
To engineer a truly decent verse.

I tried to live my nights and days,
One question at a time;
I wouldn't march the other ways:
I am a rebel; I loathe a paradigm.
But I am not a malignant narcissist:
At times, I yield; at times, I do insist.

It doesn't matter how many times I fall;
It matters how many times I get back up;
I am quite old; I often fall,
Get up, and never learn crawl.
Sincerely, Paul.

So Long

Reality is not a poker's bluff,
We had enough:
In your nostalgic eyes
I feel the warmth of our passed love
With its sun touching climbs and flies,
With its uncertainty and foggy fears,
With its abysmal dives and splashes.

Sad snowflakes melt on your lashes;
I hate the winter; I am a lonely dove.

A fat woman sang her deathly song,
She gave a performance-and-a-half;
I wonder…whether she said so long.

On my behalf.

Sorrows

She reads the half-erased tealeaves
That tightly glued to my unknown past.
She tries to trace my evident tomorrows,
My patience yields to everlasting sorrows.

Her high heels cruelly poke the virgin field of clover;
She is firmly marching over wearing the clergy cloak.

There is no time to weep; there is no place to leap,
There is no time to think, there is no place to drink,
There is no time to plea; there is no place to flee,
There is no time to talk; there is no place to walk.

I am sick and tired of her spurs,
I am sick and tired of my pain,
I am a poet, not a horse,
My verses will not die in vain.

Speculator

My guiding angel is drunken whore;
I swear, I won't obey him anymore.

I slammed through a big crowd
Of rather edgy horseracing fans;
I wished we'd win the final round,
I hoped my horses had a chance.

I was a futile speculator.

We couldn't win a single race today,
As if my fillies never left the stables.
I wolfed a burger from a paper tray
And went to wipe some other tables.

I am just a retiring waiter.

Stung

A heavy tombstone over my coffin
Doesn't allow my eager soul to rise;
I am sure it's happening quite often:
No spare rooms in the busy skies.

Depression and creativity
Forever walking hand-in-hand
Down the path of a disaster,
And at the end they walk much faster,
Just as my mare when sees her stable.

I do the same when wine is on the table.

Life's heavy-handed prick
Has broken my resistance:
I am regularly stung by love
Or by its total nonexistence,
But not in the present tense…

I bought a bucket for my final kick.

Suburban

I drank my seventh double bourbon,
Paid lazy barman and walked off.
My shiny new Suburban
Refused to start, begun to cough.
It was a final nail in my poor coffin
It happens every-so-damn-often,
I've seen this movie a few times
As price for my drunk driving crimes.

In any case, I drove her,
I was a terrible hungover,
My eyes wide-open
But I couldn't see a thing.

My heart was broken
I lost my wedding ring…

If only I could see
Her facial expression
Would send me
To a clinical depression…
Expressway and toll-free.

Sunset Will Fade

A red sunset inevitably fades just like a bullfighter's rag,
I promise to unfurl from shades the rebels' tattered flag.

The horse of time moves us ahead,
Some never get their silver spoon,
Some never get their daily bread,
Some get too much and swoon.

I am getting used to life along the slowest lane,
I had divorced my wife; she let me keep my brain.

One sparrow doesn't make a spring,
One vendor couldn't start a fair,
Although, even the mute will sing,
When life is awfully hard to bear.

Life brings me up to speed,
It offers treachery and greed;
I hope my bitterness will drain,
And I won't lose my pride in pain.

When facts get squeezed into my staggered eyes,
Life wiggles in striptease; I watch its barefaced lies.

That Cup

Most people run to lose some weight,
Although, at times, it's just an ounce;
I don't expect to bite that bait...
The others run to get elected
And then legally pounce
Upon the unsuspected.

I didn't have to wait for 9/11,
I lived a mile above the hell,
A mile beneath the heaven;
Besides, I wasn't really well...

I began getting dizzy spells,
My legs barely hold me up,
Even the churches' bells
I could no longer hear...

But I'm not ready for that cup,
I'd rather drink a case of beer.

The Cab

I am truthful through thin and thick
To every our Mother Nature's trick.

I was the lonely-only one
Still drinking in the local bar;
The barflies have already gone...
My thoughts and hopes were flying far:

Both, Eve and I were wholly naked,
The tree of knowledge was still sacred,
But sagely taught us what to do...
It was much more than we could chew.

A young bartender woke me up:
I called the cab to pick you up...

The Future's Gone

My life is lying on a chopping board,
The future's gone, the past is gored,
My shrink has failed to cure my grief'
I am falling off the cliff
On my own sword...
My final justified award.

Gold turns into the blue,
The autumns into winters;
This world is a gigantic sieve,
It doesn't forget; doesn't forgive...
My friends and I pass through,
We are the brave perpetual drifters.

My soul is flying someplace far away
Above the naked trees,
Above the gloomy clouds;
My body plows through another day,
Above the circus' crowds:
I am the red-nose clown on a trapeze...

Don't worry, at the end, I fall
I am paid to entertain you all.

The Game of Chess

We played all night,
A fight after a fight;
His Bishop took my pawn
And trapped the Queen:
My buddy beamed like dawn,
My face turned gravely green.
I was too sleepy and inept,
My baby-self-assurance wept.

I love this multilayered game
Of a complex enigmatic chess,
I didn't reach glory and fame,
But don't give up, nevertheless.

Deceptive whites and blacks
Deeply involved in vicious plots
Of shy retreats and bold attacks
Connecting cleverly the dots.

One day, I take it on the chin,
Next day, I dominate and win;
I don't anticipate the final round.
We play. Our hearts still pound.

The Leaves are Fully Turned

The blinding kindness,
The darkness of a ploy,
The weight of lightness,
The sadness of a joy.

The leaves are fully turned,
The winter pushes our door,
The lessons are not learned,
The shadows slash the floor.

Look at the amazing sight,
Look up and see the stars,
Look at the wayward Mars,
Look at the morning light.

We will survive a rainy weather,
We do not live by bread alone,
We are alive and still together,
We reap what we have sown.

The leaves are fully turned,
The lessons aren't learned.

The Olden Drawbridge is Set Apart

The olden drawbridge is set apart,
Two heartlessly alienated silhouettes,
Two loving swans were foully stopped
From executing their daily etiquettes.

They wanted just a "neck and kiss",
While a tall ship is being navigated;
They loved their silent modest bliss,
Their peace was viciously invaded.

I hope their love affair will go on,
They aren't ready for their songs,
Those melodies are yet unborn,
Until they hear the angels' horns.

The olden drawbridge is set apart
Against the gentle lights of dawns,
A fascinating masterpiece of art,
Two chiseled silhouettes of swans.

The Sun Delays its Rounds

The tablecloth of clouds slid down from the skies,
The sun delays its rounds over our tears and cries.

The history exhumes
Our tarnished times
From our dormant tombs;
The final judgment looms
Above unwritten rhymes
Still in the fertile wombs.

Times calmly paused the flights of jolly angels,
The gates are closed for all prosaic strangers.
Winds swirl between the snow-white birches,
Showing a postcard scene of our churches.

Bright as a burning match, crisp as a godsent sound,
Beyond my humble batch a rainbow taps the ground.

The sun loudly wheeled
Into my silent room;
The winter's life is sealed,
The spring must bloom.

There was a Warning Sign

I fell to six feet under to hear a looming thunder;
I climbed the wall of worry to see the lights of glory...
I swung from wrong to right to thread a single needle;
I went into a blinding night to solve that lifelong riddle.

I tried to catch a falling knife,
I tried to be a butcher's block;
I sadly lost this uphill strife
And landed on the fated rock.

There was a warning sign:
Your rain has already flowed,
Your life has already crested.
Don't ever cross the final line;
Your soul will be forever towed,
Your futile flesh will be arrested.

I knew: bad times will pass
Like sand in the hourglass;
The stars will blink and glow,
And sparkle as a virgin snow.

Those Shores

I strike the alphabet into the words
Then weave from them new worlds.

I dream of those unknown shores
Under the clouds leisurely flown
By the caressing eternity of waters
Between the metronome of oars.
At times, I see a few tossed quarters:
Some strangers keep the open doors
For their eventual return
Into those shores where sunsets burn.

Ticking

Gods canceled all my sins
Thus ending a long gap
Between my kitschy wins;
They also ended my lethargic nap...

I am a Lazarus of modern days,
I hear my loneliness in ticking clocks,
The lazy angels show me the ways
To join the churches raucous flocks...

I am not a philosopher,
I am just a hidden camera
Recording what it sees:
A death of a long love affair
Or just a sinner on his knees.

The agony of my uneven writing
Morphed into a bourgeois existence:
No daily suffering or useless fighting;
I walk the path of least resistance.

Undead

I smoked and drank a lot,
But exercised and played football;
I didn't try to split the Gordian knot,
But ran and never dropped the ball.

By chance, I outlived the friends I had;
Much later, I befriended a few new; undead…
We learned to be immune to existential despairs
We learned to place our bets on winning squares.

In our past, the knights would swear:
"I'd rather die with sword in hand…"
They used to circle every known square
And rolled them to the happy end!!!

Unwrap the Magic

Unwrap the gifts, unwrap the magic
Under the blinking Christmas tree...
Our holidays are hardly ever tragic,
I've read some classics on the shelf;
Today, I am ready to put on a show,
The time had come to please myself.

If there is a wall, there is a gate;
I pilled the wrap, I didn't hesitate;
Inside, I saw a filthy frog, I had to kiss,
But I am not a lonely girl. I live in bliss.

If there is a loaded fridge,
Only Goliath has to toss it;
If there is no bridge,
No one can cross it;
Your wife will never leave
If you don't have a wife;
So many think the Christmas Eve
Is the beginning of their happy life.

Varnished

The dusty mirrors
Don't reflect my sleepless nights,
There are no heroes
In our brawls and constant fights.

I went into the carousel of years
Through happiness and tears,
Through wars and bad divorces,
Through great and so-so verses.

The history is always tarnished
In spite of a never-ending length,
The truth is smoothly varnished;
In knowledge there is strength.

Virtuoso

She looked a little older and smarter
Than the rest of noisy gypsy thieves;
I asked whether she reads tealeaves
Then gave her fifty as a hefty starter.

My mood was crawling up and down,
But somewhere deeply underneath,
My life was like a red nosed clown
Grinding its greedy, merciless teeth.

That lady was a virtuoso; she was a real sage,
She knew my name, my problems and my age,
She promised twelve more happy years of life,
A better health, a bosom friend, a younger wife.

I am already eighty-eight,
I quickly grabbed the bait.

Whistling

I am not right off the boat,
I am no more an outlander,
I crossed an ocean, not a moat,
I didn't come here to surrender.

Sometimes, I even crack the whip
And write without any censorship.

Even my asshole whistling "Dixie"
As always for the proper reason:
I am neither shrewd nor tricksy
For life in the paradigm of prison.

Willows

For me each winter is a wound
That tries to cure itself in vain;
It is a piano never tuned,
It is a devastating pain.

The moon's inventive light
Painted the elongated shadows
On the last night's fallen fluffy snow;
The stars were vigorously blinking,
Piercing a black umbrella of the night,
And wanted us to see their sudden riot.

The frozen skies were dreadfully quiet.

Only the snowflakes were squeaking
Under my intensely unforgiving hoofs;
Only the willows were deeply weeping
Remembering their spring, their youth.

Un Cheval Volant

I am Pegasus; I am a flying horse,
In French, Je suis un Cheval Volant;
I am your muse; I am your last hurrah
In premonition of the final intercourse.
In my lifespan I learned enough,

I'll never dance you to the end of love.

Acknowledgements

I am deeply grateful to Judith Broadbent
For her uniquely skilled guidance and generous stewardship
For her unyielding yet wise editing which gives me enough space
To freely exercise my whims.

I am profoundly in debt to Dan Canale for his thoroughly detailed
And brilliant analysis and fruitful advices.

I'd like to thank Kate Broadbent
for her exquisitely nuanced suggestions and her deep
understanding of poetic imagery.

To all my friends for their genuine advice and enthusiasm.

Printed in the United States
by Baker & Taylor Publisher Services